Schizophrenia Poetry

by

M. Stefan Strozier

Published by World Audience, Inc.
(www.worldaudience.org)
303 Park Avenue South, #1440
New York, NY 10010
Phone (646) 620-7406

ISBN 978-1-934209-07-3
10-digit ISBN 1-934209-07-4

Cover art and design by Christopher Taylor

World Audience (www.worldaudience.org) is a global consortium of artists and writers, producing *audience* and *The audience Review*. Please submit stories, poems, paintings, or photography to: submissions@worldaudience.org; please send inquiries about being a reviewer to: theatre@worldaudience.org.

Schizophrenia Poetry

By

M. Stefan Strozier

A World Audience Book

(www.worldaudience.org)

April, 2010

aU Di en CE audience artist group

New York, NY

To my children, Jay and Carolyn

INTRODUCTION

The line between sanity and insanity is often a fuzzy one: perhaps almost as fuzzy as the line between truth and fiction. For most people, it's easier to get through the day-to-day busyness of modern life by drawing that line, however arbitrary, and making sure that we're on the right side of it. Those who don't seem to fit can then be classed as "other" and kept safely out of our perception. There are times when I wonder whether we don't fill our lives with non-contemplative activity solely for the purpose of avoiding the kind of intense contemplation that could easily pitch any of us, whatever our "classification," into a world that appears, at the very least, unsettling. Unfortunately, for those brave readers who have picked up this collection, it isn't going to be so easy to maintain that sense of differentiation. The poems in M. Stefan Strozier's *Schizophrenia Poetry* tend to pull the reader directly into the beating heart of madness. There are hallucinations, fear, paranoia, darkness, and pain, but it isn't all negative. There is also pleasure, wonder, and even, at times, a sense of superpower as the poems move beyond the abyss towards the creation of a viable perception.

Allow yourself to be taken into the poems, and at times you'll find yourself lost in Strozier's maze, face to face with a deadly Minotaur; but not without Aradne's thread. Keep your wits about you and you'll emerge in light. *Schizophrenia Poetry* is full of poems that touch on insanity certainly, shedding light on the daily struggle for simple survival that a schizophrenic might face. But they are more than that. The poems in this book will change the way you perceive what can only be called, in this instance at least, an altered consciousness rather than an illness in search of a cure. But they also touch on something common and familiar, the work collectively slouching towards a sense of order and reason. The poet's search is everyman's search: for meaning, for justice, for sanity, and above all, for self-knowledge. After reading these it is impossible to simply distance yourself from the schizophrenic poet who forms the narrative "I" in this work, or to point a finger and say that this is something unknowable, untenable, or plain old "mad". The spectrum or continuum along which Strozier's poetry moves is one that will be immediate to all readers whether they've struggled with the fickle flashings of the mind or not. Poems like "Waking Dreams" or "Scream" are familiar enough dream landscapes. Others like "The Heights", or "Voices" could just as easily be read as the pain of depression, desire, or any artistic longing as a struggle with hallucination. The final poems in the book muse on the nature of poetry itself, and the poet's role as seer, truth seeker and truth maker and end the book on a very positive note.

There is order in Strozier's art, and a strong literary heritage that calls up Dante, Greek mythology, Blake (as any poetry which deals with visions does), Vonnegut, and even tainted icons of modernity: Quentin Tarantino, Bob Marley, and Sponge Bob Square Pants (a character that would give anyone nightmares).

Many of the poems are acrostic, self-referential, and heavily invested with rhythm and sound. Although there is certainly an air of seriousness about the work, there is also humour, as in the Bukowski inspired "Rugby Scrum" which brings literary "hard hitters" together in for a game of football. "8 Prepositions" gives the reader a lovely little poem of sardonic grammar, or "Charlie Rose", which explores the writer's struggle for recognition in a talk show world. The metaphors are strong and original, the work thoughtful, wrought, powerful, and in the end, positive in their approach to what some might consider a debilitating topic, never mind condition. Strozier never lets either the schizophrenia or the pain diminish what he is aiming for: those poetic moments which achieve transcendence.

—*Magdalena Ball*

The Compulsive Reader, http://www.compulsivereader.com, 2006

Paranoia

I am going mad,
In this room,
In front of this computer screen,
Following these words,
Along this page.
This is a regular event.
I am mildly bothered by it.
I do not think you understand.
There are things,
Slithering under the door,
And hiding in the shadows
And, the omnipresent,
Government spies are
Watching me
Despite this logic:
"Who cares?"
The aliens, however,
Are most certainly observing
Me and the government spies.
In this era,
There are also regular people
Watching me
They're watching you, too.

I am watching you,
My dear.

Waking Dreams

There was a time when
I did not have anywhere
I could call home
I was awake because
Sleeping was difficult
Well, after several weeks,
I entered the world of dreams.
I spent a lot of time in the library,
Reading,
Writing poems, like this one,
Observing,
As a huge black fly
Flying around the room,
Before slamming into my right eyeball;
Two gold dragons in the bushes,
On the other side of the glass –
Beyond them, hiding,
A praying mantis is poised to strike,
The dragons.
A cockroach, three feet long,
Moves toward me,
Scurrying across the table
Now it is on my jacket,
Crawling up my sleeve
Voices scream,
Over a unknown sound system
Turning to listen,
I see there is nothing there
(The voices are there.)
Forms are morphed into other things:

A headless astronaut –
Also speaking,
A giant snake,
Patterns on the floor,
The ceiling, the walls, my eyeballs.
Rather than diminish,
These things grow, exponentially –
Each image, scraping a fork across a plate of china,
Inside my brain.

Here,

Follow me,

This is the place,

Beyond the abysses;

I see clearly through fogs,

Where backwater channels,

Struggling against time,

And cosmic forces,

Desire not sleep;

But to meet,

And flow,

Forever

Where

Both

Death

And reality

Are mired, sloshing,

And mirrored are dreams,

And imagination, as it should be.

It is in that place I am now

And, when I arrive here,

I never want to leave.

Perhaps, you can

Understand me

I only want

To stay

Lost

For all

Eternity –

Perhaps, you

Cannot understand;

For you, only two things

Are certain – and no more:

Reality and its banal clichés –

For, if you would simply allow

Your mind to sail through, you

Might make it to where I am –

Maybe, not quite as close;

But nearby;

I'll watch

For you.

A Moment

Trees rustling, daytime –
Raining; dark clouds, scattering –
Relief for waning hopes
Setting sun breaks through,
Even it is blocked.
Human cries,
Car brakes, screeching,
Buses hiss
There is no end,
No answer   nor, justice:
Reason or purpose.

I dropped this piece of paper,
From a window
On the sixth floor –

Apparently, someone has found it

Scream

I hope we weather this storm
Weather the storm weather the storm
Whipping through the hollows
Screaming for recognition
In my heart
In my weary heart in my weary heart
And your tired eyes and your tired eyes
I can see in the storm
Searching like the wind,
For harbor in my arms
I hope we weather this storm
You and
I

Free Verse

Pausing for a moment,
Writing in my diary,
Bored of pained torment,
A demon, red and fiery

Slowly rose above my soul –
Succubus, she once was my muse
Too long I paid her high toll;
I have the power to choose

Confusion left my mind
How can I live without her?
She was cruel and unkind;
But she made my pen purr

Now, there is only hard, cut form
I created a new, sculpt whole
Without shelter, I am the storm – a
Unbendable, magical soul.

Home

Leaving the train,
Walking inland,
To find my soul
And my self,
In this bustle and hustle
Seem to have
Come up missing,
Many a year now
Searching for that place,
Once called home

Memories flash like lightning,
Swaying weeds, and strangeness,
All the same
Refilled distant voids
And slow, cold, corn syrup,
On hard pancakes
This ordinary place,
I see is like all the rest

A cats vexing gaze,
Enters my mind for an instant –
There; but not
Uninvited
Standing in the cold wind
A storm is coming
The weatherman said
Snowflakes start to blow past my face
Squinting my eyes,
Mornings past, waiting,

For my father
Hands numb now, waiting,
For release,
From this cold,

Cold,

Someone else's home.

Snowy Ridge

I wrote some poems and saved them on floppy disks
And a few were lost,
Along with some stories.
I have lost a lot of work over the years
I guess it is inevitable for every writer
There is, perhaps, nothing in life worse
Than losing a poem or a story
You tend to remember it
The way you remember good things;
Still, this poem had meaning
Because at the time I wrote it,
I was starving
In the day, I went to a university library –
It was open for some reason –
in Las Vegas.
I would spend the whole day there,
Reading and writing in a cubicle,
On the top floor
It was at a certain point of my development as a writer,
When I put my heart into my words,
Before I leaned how to cut my heart with a scalpel,
In order for my heart to bleed effectively,
In the darkest of colors.
In the morning, I would look across the city,
See tiny people and cars and houses,
In the distance, there was a snowy ridge,
Its miniscule valleys, trees
Roads, disappearing into the trees;
Houses to either side, scampering up the base;
But mostly there was only the snowy ridge,

Stretching straight across the skyline,
Jagged, all alone

I have never been one to get sentimental;
But did I ever want to be at the top of that mountain

The Heights

In wandering up to an overlook,
Where the sky is clear and blue,
And birds circle high in the air
The city stretches into distance,
Abated by treed hillsides
I am welcomed here,
By no one and nothing
The river is to my left –
Strong; but barely discernable –
Behind me, there is a tourist castle.
I smile at the secret I hold.

The Graveyard

This poem is written in 69 rhyming, heroic couplets. Many lines have additional, internal rhymes. The couplets alternate between six and nine syllables. Both lines, of every couplet, follow the exact same metrical pattern. The patterns of every couplet are different. This poem was written immediately following the 9-11 attack on America and took years to finish.

uando noe fummo fatti tanto,
ch'al mio maestro piacque di mostarmi
la creatura ch'ebbe il bel sembiante,

d'innanzi me si tolse e fe restarmi,
"Ecco Dite," dicendo, "ed ecco il loco
ove convien che di fortezza t'armi."

Com'io divenni allor gelato e fioco,
mol dimandar, lettor, ch'I'non lo scrivo,
pero ch'ogne parlar sarebbe poco.

Io non mori'e non rimasi vivo;
pensa oggimari per te, s'hai fior d'ingegno,
qual io dicenni, d'uno e d'altro privo

(Canto XXXIV, Dante's *Inferno*)

At the edge of the universe, there's a low wall
All of poetry's verse could not fathom how tall

But, if you surmount it, 'long it you'd walk, never ever reaching tomorrow
Longer than the sleeping, white-eyed dead stalk, whose dreams of sorrow you should borrow

The wall's windward, forever; leeward, end of time
Just like paintings sever; so too, limits this rhyme

And there, if you get hopelessly lost, listless drift, as your mind's darker side,
Appears to have a violent cause – seems to rift; nay, it cries, *'I have died.'*

§ § §

I see two horsemen, with starry cloaks, heavy cowls;
I say (so low), "I'm sorry;" and, let loose my bowels

These predators of weak and weary; I see under hoods, keen eyes fiery
A premonition…poppies, heavy as my heart – sinking, red – twists wryly

'Click-clack' – slow-pace – to my face; speaking, gargle-voic'd,
"Cold tears race, laced with the imagined lie they're moist;

"you are a pall pawn, locked within a cosmos endless: time's sad capsule.
In this outer ring, hell is oblivion; and darkness, evil's vestibule.

"This illusion is made master by feeling pain,
as confusion is blanketing your eyes like rain,"

One says; and, grasps for his whip; 'crack,' round around tight, the leather bounds…"Oh, please!"
Now, he pulls reins to his black shoulder; I kick, dragging my feet, rasping knees

Cold assails, as Hades' teeming, blinding blizzards
Horror tales; demon statues; gargoyle wizards –

Carved iron, bronze and gold and silver; wyvern, imp and hell's chimera;
Battles, executions, souls a burn, adorn each massive, metal vista

My dread, it lingers, finding two – three – broke fingers;
Now, distant doorbell ringers; strange bird malingers

The filth and dirt I taste on tip of tongue; in corners, black snow pack'd in place
With laughing rage a rider's flung his hood – an undead, smiling face

"Fools! What have you done to this…this…there's only one?
Oh! I will have you…run!…both put in the hot sun!"

My vision is fading peacefully, lying facedown, in a wide courtyard,
Some twenty or thirty voices are talking *insanely* in this psyche ward.

§ § §

I wake to incense, pearls; the tapestries unfurl
A candleholder curls: soft, delicate whirl

A purple, ripe, half-bitten plumb, on top of burgundy-cream mitten
The silk is black; and, sternly written, stare eyes, speaking desires smitten

In thistle bed narcosis, nestling nightingale
'I'm gonna shoot my wad Θ the spliffs!' – more voices rail

I feel stinging pain of release – don't resist – oh…If I dreamt in day…
She's a consistency…grease; and, then speaks (I have not the breath to say),

"Your name? – I'm Persephone, the wife of the devil."
I get up quick; and, moan, huskily level

I see two doors – one red, near the bed; one black – far – near faded tapestry
So I bolt, dead ahead, as a colt, I, myself, am told, *'no causality.'*

"I'm glad you came!" she exasperatedly pleads;
"I love you," pines she, made tame – mounting tension seethes

"I fear you, all the same," I mumble, grasping, turning, shiny brass handle;
And, knocking down some of the candles, stumble; lying, "Hey! My name's Randal!"

Door flies open; and, into a looming, dark hall –
– tight gloom; senses are booming; my leopard claws mall.

§ § §

"Hello? Is someone there?" I remand; but there comes no reply – (someone's where?)
(Sometimes, I survey one lone petal's edge, of a red rose; and, love is there.)

"Narcissus." He's lit a match; and, a torch flames
He's a silent mime; I watch, as the ash rains

"Do you know of…?" (Loathing for whom confusion is – like – a lot of lipsticks.)
"Yes; you are referring to your goddess? She's a concubine, with two dicks."

"At least a married woman and I didn't dine!"
"That's – like – assumin'. Go that way, for *labyrinth time*!"

The tunnel is six feet wide; and, rocky dirt, like coal miners' shafts – (I know)
He walks on the left side; turning aft, I see light close quick (a boat I row)

I trip on an adz, curse in full; and, wipe my brow
"Pasiphae loves bull – knife let – out comes no cow.

"Daedalus, word architect, built labyrinth – mind-like – nineteen hundred four; and,
Inside: horns, hoofs, curding straw rind, Minotaur huffs, puffs; and, goes where I plan."

I ask this iconoclastic idol, "Who am I?"
"Well, fantastic," he says; and, his ending is now nigh,

"You're the Master of Insanity; the Schizophrenic Man of Letters." ۞
I disappear into a porthole; as kindly manatee unfetters;

Popping out: confused, dull-witted, slow to roll;
Standing, I bemuse, clear sight is in my soul.

§ § §

The walls are tall; torches are alight up high; the rest almost pitch black
I step ahead, tight, my three left fingers rap; the rising heat, harsh blast ╬
I walk, trying to stall my rising fear at bay ╠
I turn corners; and, meet small t; three choices lay ╩
I go right, due to easier rhyme; and, now I hear a faint, sweet, pure music ╝
The off-beat sharp, on certain notes; but in slow time; the song rolls strong ♫
reggae [sic]

Slithering through number 4; then, lettered L ╥ ╙
Gliding along, like a silent whore…what the hell? ╬

It's Bob Marley! – wailing *Running – hell ° bent – Away* on golden 6-string g'tar
"Come ere, rude boy," → thus, I'm sent to him, hypnotiz'd by melodic rebar

"Dread naught, dread; weak is drawing dreadnaught; but dem smote,
Speak jah boy's speak: Every need got ego feed it,"

Says he, vanishing in full; suddenly, bursting the void, is a creature
With a bottom of a man – torso a bull, I run faster than future

The bull is pursuing – gaining – what says prophet?
"Oh, Narcissus – you are flow'ring – ya'know, I'd bet…"

The beast rams his horn between my legs, hoists me – I speak prayers to a deaf god
The bull stops; and, flings rudely I → gold door, I see; and, standing…a spent rod

"Charon, pausing ferry: he admires, adores you,
muses came to bury; they found your stem in dew."

§ § §

On the other side is chaos → tongue-tied turquoise giraffes canter, cripple
Lovely maidens Bacchus calls to; someone Claude, insects, demons, worms in apples

Ocelots gnawing Nazi orgies; maelstrom rules
Overhead, pterodactyl sorties fly in schools

Atta is being pluck'd by praying mantis, his soul rent into tiny pieces;
Gone, his religion, eyes; the shade is lying in sad sorrow – it's his own feces

I search for the path, desiring leave – no séance
Though curiosity's wrath, it lies and taunts

Through the mindless confusion, I hear again the soothing voice of prowess
It is lion. He says, "How you doin', rude boy? Look: Ahead is fortress;
⇧

now, we'll fly over Dis, so you can meet you: *It.*"
Reckon; Jah's magic bliss is carry'ng… mind … seize … fit …

§ § §

I open my eyes → darkness; I step slow; and, a strong pair of – I think – hands…
I'm shackled in cold, stale room to hard bed; and, I groan low – these are harsh
lands

I yonder see a slim yellow moon sequester'd
I ponder, feeling – well – mellow, tar'd and feathered

Now is rising, back of mind, a voice resounding, beyond walls of fogs
Like the sound of double redound, voic'd of ship's horns, within ancient peat bogs

"Who is speaking to me? What's happening in here?
Listen, ghost! I am me, not we – you keep your fear!"

"I'm touch'd, branded – seem so beholden – to have you near; all's forgotten
Things best, us between – you, me – even-and-Steven, you, which I've begotten…"

"Listen, you – a-k-a – me; it's time us two we
talk; I am so…á la…oh….it's wrong to woo thee…."

"Ah ha! Into middle mind's eye comes a little riddle – where are fiddles?
Precede kings and bridle, camping sites and dragons, what by? Compounds?
Titles?"

"The enemy of nouns! I win; but lived sin
to deserve evil kin; (he crawls beneath my skin.)"

"You getting feisty, precious little bitch? Why don't you shut it! Guards, seize him!"
"You are a witch! Hey, wait! There's something happ'ning here!" I'm yelling hoarse,
wits dim

I've grown fangs; lapping my skin is tiny red flames;
Gnaw, rip, tear, shackles away as tin; I toss reigns

I throw a leather strap around a neck; I hear it pop – a loud pa-snap!
Un-hog my strap, I rope lasso a peck: A rabbit, snake has tied in wrap

Squeeze *It* to death, just like Dr. Octopus;
Exploding lab of meth; spilling down couscous

Raising my arms up high, I am yelling, "Never clangor; and, thus ranker, neither from Burma, Bangladesh, Bangor, Budapest,...the Duppy Conqueror!"

§ § §

I lie still, drained, like a dry gin mill's still
My will beat, barren; I've my fill, *Kill Bill*'s pill

From down the hall, undead and painful screams: loud and grating reality
These are the dead, you, who approaches here; strange are words of painful rhapsody

Ten thousand years hence, you'll not read this – or, if so,
Say, "Simply mad, he, since minds craz'd, logic can't sow."

Here's a lunatic; yet, perhaps only truth survives; for, where are your words?
This is one more question: evil truth; are humans a thing of God's words...?

Down icy waters I drown, driven mad by sounds
And, freezing cold, now my heart, ever-slower pounds

.

.

.

.

.

.

.

.

.

.

.

.

.

.

Flying

For years,
I have tried to fly

I flew in my dreams;
But always,
Stopping short,
Fearing,
Doing wrong
The physics held me back,
At first;
However, I conquered those
(It took some time.)

I thought I could –
Mechanically, at least,
Take flight
I reasoned,
If I pushed my machine
Fast enough,
It too, would take flight;
It was preposterous;
But
Worth a try
On the first trial,
I pushed, down the runway,
Cutting and scraping myself,
Along the way
I had moved
Some people gathered,
To watch and laugh

This routine continued,
For a long time,
Over and over
Nothing seemed to happen –
Really,
Nothing, at all;
Until one day,
Just as they say,
With a red bandana on my forehead,
Bruised, bloodied –
My engine skipped,
Sputtered;
And –
Suddenly,
It took flight

I could not believe it
Something must be wrong;
In fact, everything
Was horribly wrong;
Except, there was no denying,
I was in the air
And flying
The people,
Little specks, on the ground
Birds regarding me
As equal
(Though with some trepidation.)
Lightning,
Narrowly missing me,
I had to avoid other aircraft,
As my machine
Ripped through the blue sky
I thought:

This is it?
This is all there is to flying?
Just moving along, through the air?

Nothing
Is as painful as it seems,
After the fact

The Sheriff

Kid Mila rode into town
It was early
They saw him coming,
And kept firing at him;
But Kid Mila outsmarted 'em all,
Firing back with his six guns –
He won.
The sheriff and the lawmen
Were long gone from the dusty town,
And there was nothing; but
Lawlessness

Well.

Kid Mila, right away,
Fired up the place
And went in the bar
Calling out for Whiskey
Double
The barkeep served him proper
Kid Mila drank the glass,
Slammed it on the bar;
Then, he saw an old man,
Drinking at the other end of the bar;
So, Kid Mila said to him,
"Hey, old man,
what the hell's wrong with this place?"
The old man said, "I'm afraid
everything has been dead here
for over forty years."

"That long? –
(There was a pause.)

I'm a poet!" Kid Mila said.

"Longer," the old man replied.

Well,
Kid Mila finished his drink
And rode out to camp,
Got himself a gal
By name o Lady Persephone,
A few drinking buddies,
A second-hand computer,
A third-rate job –
And sometimes no job,
And a box –
Became a regular
At the low-down bars
The town began
To get wise to Kid Mila
Every time the townsfolk got lazy –
Well, Kid Mila,
He'd start shooting up the place
Well,
One day,
Kid Mila swung out 'a the bar,
Stumbling,
After drinking all night
It was daylight,
When the town crier
Came running up, and said,
"Kid Mila! They done stolt
your horse 'an both 'a your mules,

shot your dog plum dead;
plus, your gal's – well, she's with the perpetrator(s)."
"They shot my dog?"
"Yep."
"Don't these townsfolk have a strand of decency?
"Nope."
"They'll pay for shooting my dog."
"Whatcha gonna do, Kid Mila?"
Kid Mila said,
"It's a sad town ain't got no poets, brother.
It's a sad town.
But, the world's done gone global,
and I don't need to hang around here anymore
to prefect my craft; or, for much of anything,
for that matter.
I'm tired of it, and I'm leaving."
"So, you leaving, Kid Mila?
Huh?" The town crier whined.
"Yes, I am going down to Central America,
and I ain't coming back.
The women are prettier, dance better;
And, a poet can write his words in peace,
without them being stolen."
"Bye, Kid Mila."

But,
As Kid Mila was walking away,
The town crier said,
"I guess Vonnegut was right 'bout you."
"What?"
"Mr. Kurt Vonnegut – he's from parts back east,
and he said you're the running kind
'narry staying in one place for too long,
'cause you get mad and pout off like a baby –

he said watch out for you.
that's what Vonnegut said about you."
Kid Mila said,
"Well, you tell Mr. Vonnegut
I will *keep* running too –
until I get it right;
and, then we'll see what happens."

So Kid Mila walked into the sunset,
And the desert,
Because he did not have a horse
Anymore,
Or money for a new horse
After about four miles of tired walking,
Kid Mila turned around,
And went back to the low-down bar.

Hard Turn

Once, I rode in a sailboat
To the timeless end of space
A sea ahead of me, like a moat;
And I found myself in a race

I pulled hard, locked rudder in place;
There, finally, saw what must be end

All at once, my soul and body rent;
And, I collapsed to the ground, spent.

Life, at times, seems too distant;
My vision, a hazy implant

Any sense I attempt, a simple rant:
Is there a thing, other than hope?
Against all, I want to know and can't
I ask the beyond – the reply comes, "Nope."

Voices

Speak in silent voices to my mind
I do not ignore the speech from within
The silent words tear my soul, the words
The words envelop my soul
Voices unceasing, unquiet
Too loud in my mind, like a chapel
Full of rude people, talking in loud voices
To be heard, those an unconscious does not want
To hear, and they do not relent for me,
A man, in sheets of rain, fear envelops
Weak uncertainty, foreboding, coldness –
Do you not believe me? – they speak, my friend
Do they not speak to me?

I hear a woman softly say, whispering,
"I seem to mean I dream, as screeching bells
envelop night air, wishing death upon
all things."
A man talks loudly, "Can a span of time,
encompass seven words and rhymes?
we bore down on the scoundrels one night,
up lead ship's battle orders went, darkness,
shrouded the ocean and the sky above –
then, flash and cannon fire above the water
and answered, on and on it went, coughing,
as Cerberus' bark, at he who enters Hades
alive and red lightning, skipping over
glistening waters – hellfire, pushing the shot –
ahead, slow enough for a man's eye, cruel enough
to remember in dreams and nightmares –

run, and it will give chase, feeding off lust
for your mind
I am scared to die, he said,
and he died in my arms,
as I cradled his dead skull –
death, the very face of it – there is nothing but coldness."

And on through the night,
And into the day,
Never sleeping,
Never dreaming
Wash away my soul,
Wash away my existence,
Into the night,
Into the storm

Scarecrow

Flying over a rise,
Beating red wings, black wings
Tiny feathers drop to the ground
In a world where dying are dead,
It is sad to know love
Mind steady as a rudder in the deep green sea,
As white froth splits the ocean apart
In a cool evening,
The oddity stays affixed to a pole
In the center of a field
All of God's creatures fear the unknown – except,
One fearing what is imagined: The Scarecrow.
And, he reigns in my imagination
For forever
And anon

Charlie Rose

For years,
I have allowed myself one fantasy,
I wanted to be interviewed on Charlie Rose,
As a great writer
You see:
I had first written poetry during high school,
To help regain my mind, after going insane
I also wrote stories; and, then I wrote a book in my early twenties,
And another after I returned from war;
So, by my late twenties, I was writing like mad
Much of it is gone
Married with 3 kids,
I was attending 3 universities and working full-time;
But I was still writing
My only pleasures: A bowl of cereal each night – well,
It was more like the whole box
And a gallon of milk; and, the Charlie Rose show

One writer had said:
"Well, all a writer must do is write."

Do not remind me of this,
Or punctuation or structure or grammar!

A wise and powerful bear
Now crawls through my mind
Unsatisfied and devouring,
This creature moves in shadows
With ease and silence,
Invisible to everyone else

This bear does not belong in my age
He is crude and hostile –
No one fears or hears him
The bear's roar is as loud as he makes it,
Or there is silence

As you can see,
I won't be able to appear on Mr. Rose's TV show

8 Prepositions

On the 9th floor, I asked a stranger,
"Where is that broken elevator, which,
I stepped from out of –
From down to up – at?"
He replied, "My God, man – you've just said a sentence, ending in 8 prepositions!"
"Thank you," I said humbly, continuing down the steps.

Ode to a Firing Squad

Ancient, pale, abyssal, whitewashed froth
Covering stallion He rides on through hell
Comes mine own master, in darkest night's cloth
Death rides nigh at I, for who tolls the bell
Blackness – remain strong – no one is with me
Michael, silence mind, row with abandon
Now, forlorn, are the happy times of old
Shackled wrists, sweat-blinded eyes, that can't see
Those blurred images, loaded at random
Eye for an eye, as the Good Book has told

Dealers of death, stealers of God's vision
Is justice dispensed with you caliber?
Aim now at heart and mind with precision
God's true coy assassin, the mockingbird
Perched, yonder dead tree, O irony
Smoking deep a last cigarette, the rush
Softly floods fear so near, moments, too clear
Howling, sad truth slowly slips out from me
Killer's eyes shed my reality's touch
My arteries pump the feel of my fear

The misty morning blights out sunlight's love
High above, screaming black crow, I hear it
In moments, will begin flight of a dove
I had wanted something else, God damn it
A mind suddenly awake to color,
Paused, haunted, tainted, by dark suspicion
Because it's I who is about to die, today –
Emotions sad, thoughts move deftly duller

Sing just once more now silent musicians
Before mine soul has nothing more to say

Cold October morn', I welcome death's pain
Ungainly end, grating the nerves of fate
My eyes will diminish, and pain will wane
All of Life's lies, it is you, which I hate –
Now, to you killers I speak honest:
Your country, naught but angry hypocrites,
Leaders, solely, throw lives at enemies;
And, own countrymen happily molest,
Ignorant, you follow this government,
My peace said, soul readied with two pennies

Bullets killing, splintering temple's bone
Palpitating heart, sputtering, gulps life
Spilling on concrete prisoner camp stone
Flickering tongue of devil's shining knife
Beasts of the night, my terror your bedlam
Black crow's song cut off, from the bullet's fight,
Only Devil can sing so beautiful
Flying over, crying out, He led them,
Sorrow, shudder away fear of the night,
My seething blood makes a purple pool-full

No Grecian urn – only a firing squad
The way things ought to be done, decisive
No naked wrestlers – a corpse, shoes well-trod
In witnessing death, pain, and other vices
For centuries, nothing changing for man,
No further than Alice's rabbit hole;
The end of this confused race draws near,
For naught was learned this day, in this land;
And, a black crow, paying Charon's toll,
Returns to sip unmoving eyes' last tear

Are The Wolves Going To Attack?
(A tribute to poet John Knoepfle)

A Distant howl rode on chilling black night
Cro-Magnon might have sensed looming danger
Hell's evil awakened in my mind's sight
Plainly, I could see this was no stranger
My memory dumbly speaking of past
Images, strange numbness in nightmare
Beasts seeking longingly and steadfast
Once I entered dreams of their own lair
Waiting; the rain steadily beats in down in sheets, but to move I do not dare.

Howls seek a tainted life of sickness and woe
Happy childhood – void, strange, adult life
Succulent Prince, amongst ancient foe
I've His courage to end a life of vice
Struggling for my soul to be stillborn,
Stare into black box to have never begun
My feet are kept here, for lives lost I morn
This I desire not, wishing the race done
Everything here and now is forever gone and by me the world is shun.

Only one thought is calm, surely must be
Everyone's eyes I soul-begotten meet
To fathom the depths of sky and stars
Feeling wind, standing in field of wheat
I scream, for I do not know my own sight
In black eyes, I seek my restful desire
To see as others, making my mind right
Comfort of earth, water, air and fire
I strangle the neck of Persephone to win favor of my own sire.

Oh God, I long have ran from adversaries
Nearing wolves, the voices, and I so weak
Looking up from coffin, my soul she buries –
She, the wife of zombies who walk as meek,
Arms outstretched, traveling forwards
Whipping heads around in frantic trances
Numbing fear, as sailors who walks the boards
Through sockets of my skull crawl red ants,
One and all, you dumb, numb idiots of the night, on my grave dance.

The big one, his choking breathing, I hear
He, always keener, with white, sharpened teeth
Drooling blood – whose is it? Approaching near,
I run corridors, like a guilty thief
Pairs of red eyes pursue, close in attack,
Seeking rotting marrow and diseased heart
Again a howl, unholy answered back
To keep dignity, with life gladly part
To the end, this hellish nightmare navigates from an all-too-familiar chart.

In a stagnant pond, pausing in a wood
I look heavenward, drizzling rain my view
Thoughts move to a time unknown, I could
Be an eaten carcass in morning dew;
For, now my wish in this nightmare, it seems,
Their growling is mocking courage I lack
To end this life I cannot find in dreams
Here, at last, I am free from the wolf pack
Peace, in the solitude of dark, lonely night, for the wolves have attacked.

Closing in, from impregnable birch forest
Low white eyes, from childhood nightmare
They converge, my heart skips, seeing no test
I jump and splash the water, like a hare
This action incites them, with love to kill
One bites thick muscle of my calf, his teeth
Sink into flesh, the pain I feel, until,
Waiting for death, my red blood does seethe
I am dying before mine own eyes, to an unknown God, my soul I bequeath.

I see a man through tunnels of my fear
Reaching the end, I am slacking
In darkness of night, a judgment draws near
A horse's shoes are heard click-clacking
My flesh, in bloody chunks, the wolves tore
Eyes wide, like a dying deer, lamented
Pious thoughts are no help, I am a whore
As a Viking's eagle, I am dissected
I am neither alive nor dead, past nor present, as high above, in dark clouds,

Lastly, I could see vultures had descended.

Poetry

Poetry is
Connecting
Each word
With a feeling,
And then,
Back again,
Which is why,
You
Are
Tangling
With
A
Tarantula.

A Monument

I went to a Monument; there I saw
Huge wings, reaching in a blue sky;
People gathered round; and, looking
Up to the sky, I licked an evil taste
On my tongue's tip: Will life end?
Not to be forgotten, those people,
Mockingly, outflanked the windstorm;
Screaming like muted angels, spitting,
In the dust of generations; and, I can't
Remember anymore of a Monument,
The birds of prey, silencing dreams;
Who waves for hope, or goodbye?
Maybe, I can hear a distant wind.
Meeting a disfiguring gaze,
All of time is reflected –
Then, the people,
Came home,
From their ways,
They would go see
A Monument; but lo –
A Monument was gone.
Weeping and gnashing teeth,
There is a man, reeling in pain,
His kidneys are being eaten;
Every night, ever-after,
He is screaming.
And, I remembered
A monument; I smiled also,
Feeding my pregnant wife flesh,
I was satisfied like the eagle –

The second bird returned;
And, it made me sick,
Feasting twice,
On the soul
Of a man.
Scarred,
I slept, and slowly,
Loosening my chokehold –
In the night came the demons –
Dreams dripped, starving my mind,
Violent as I had squeezed day
There is no more to say.
Lives in other times,
Feel sorrow,
And pain.

Knowingly smirking, those
Mad people then smashing
A Monument and America
Gazing at a face of massive cancerous lesions,
Becoming unbound, I swam to the brave home
I went all the way to the bottom, wanting no air
It was there I saw a Monument and saw an evil
Look deep in those pit eyes; you will see a flag…

The sun's rays split the skyscrapers of New Amsterdam
The rain weakly cleaning the grime away
Reeking there on sandy shores,
Smoldering rubble funeral pile
The broken stone piled vast
The same eagle of bronze
Looks out at the harbor
And when I stare deep
In pit eyes, I can see

More than just
End of all time
I can see the
Arriving
Bird
Dawns
A new era.

Rugby Scrum

(Inspired by a Charles Bukowski poem about baseball.)

Hemingway: get in at weak side lock
You always choke under pressure,
But who else is there?
Bukowski: strong side lock
Keep it lively in the scrum
Ginsberg: get in there at hooker
And get your feet around the ball
Second row: Homer and Dante
Flankers are crazy, not a lot of imagination:
Joyce and Kerouac;
Joyce on the inside
8-man is usually high on himself:
Gertrude Stein, you've got big shoulders;
Besides, with a woman, we'll take any ties
Scrum-half, tossing the ball from forwards backs:
Poe, you're quick on your feet
Fly-half, the leader, the QB (of the backs, anyway):
Twain
Inside center, aggressive, with a mean streak:
Faulkner
Outside center must think defensively,
A back like a forward:
Tolstoy
Scrum-side wing, in his own world –
Scores because he's ignored:
Marquez
Fullback: last line of defiance
An iron man: Whitman
Backside wing, quick, light, deadly;

And, can win a game for a team:
Fitzgerald
Pound, you can be my assistant, drawing up plays

This team is invincible
There will be other teams in the future;
And man,
What a party after the game.

Hey! Mr. Blind, One Eyed Giant, Nobody Tricked Me Too! (Or, The Ramblings of a Madman)

Just once, I was upon time,
In a land far, far and a ways away from here
Where Somewhere and Nowhere were both together there
I was be and know where just where there was
And Nobody was coming after me,
I swear to God, He was
Alice was here, too
Bring that little bitch back
For I hath loaned her a Benjamin, to get by
Whom was there, with her, and the hare, over there?
Nobody is who, among The-Them-there-two, too
I: a soul breathing life, like a holy, wholly, woken, wooly, mastodon
Immaculately emancipated (bit emaciated), en-masse, from immense, amassed, massy, mass
"Let the game begin, egad!"
I whispered out to Nobody, in particular
I ran across the bridge, spanning New Dis City, below
Turned and awaited for Nobody, to close in on me
Nobody was not there, trust me, this could I see
Nor was He there, however, either, neither
I am only so sure of It –
Not so sure about That –
I'll be clearer about That later – Not – just As; of Yet
As; of Yet, is – and always will be – just a friend
We go away backwards, even if he is queer as a three dollar bill
Still, As; of Yet, always and forever, will be where It is
(At; the Time, his `cus he `casionally rolls with.)
Was this Nobody harmless like a dog?
Jumping over backwards on its ass?

Do you know what I mean?
Do you do do? I won't go anywhere there
Wouldn't be prudent at this juncture
Suddenly, It dawned down upon me
Son-of-a-bitch must have been hiding in the fire escape complex
Was this It Nobody's evil, double negative twin, Somebody?
I was left uncertain, so I reached back with my lithe right,
Handedly threw It to the ground,
Sundered sundry quandaries asunder suddenly bummed me
Its Sunday morning
Irregardlessly, It withered
"I am It, not That."
I saw my opportunity and went for It:
"Fellow, you should take out word insurance
because I am nearing pimp-slappage upon your verbiage, with my massive diction,
as I am Not, Somebody!
if I were you, I would say: 'I am Somebody!'
but I am Not, so I say, 'I am Not!' –
am I Not, Anybody, either? –
negatron, I am neither either Not, nor am I Not, either neither
neither am I either, nor am I neither, either
no, all is Not for naught,
more then double 00 I got, damn, I'm hot
my God, what have my hand's wrought?
say, you ought to jot,
I am Not, you idiot;
get it through your knotty scull,
whom, ever the hell you are –
Well, of time
It had marched on
I paused, on cobblestone street corner
Mist exiting my nostrils like an angry triceratops
Sensing the big one coming soon

Now let me now say this about That
Typical, complicated woman,
My chances of figuring out, slim to none
Slim, just having caught the last E train out of town
Still, That is a good thing, got That?
I never got to get any of That,
If you must know That,
Know that That establishes That –
That dislikes That –
To be *established,* for That *is*
Nobody can establish That, too; however –
Wait just one second, will you look at That?
Serendipitously, I breathed a sigh of relief,
Fog channeling out my pie hole like a dragoon –
Perhaps, I too, had just established That
Spying an open field, I ran out, into the middle,
Yet again, fast turning into my rear area, I shout:
"Show yourself, Nobody."
(A. Long Pause – this old guy, wandering lonely,
Taking time away the only way he knows, passes.)
"Who are you?"
"What do you mean, who I am?"
"Maybe beware of being beware of whom you may be;
For, if you don't know who you are,
Nobody will hunt you down until Nobody is you."
I stood there agape at this giant's gap in logic,
Faintest rays of sunlight piercing,
The misty morning air
Hushed police sirens in the distance –
Nobody was gone

Poems

Flashes of distant lightning
Sounds of rolling thunder
Is how poems arrive
The action is instantaneous
When consciousness returns,
It is dimly lit,
As a distant shoreline,
Of flickering lights,
In a wan skyline
Of black night
And its jagged edges

The poet rides in a little rowboat,
The boat pulls into the town's harbor
Water sloshes the boat's wet wood
Fog horns call the night
Bells jingle softly
An enormous ship passes,
Going to the ocean
What is the darkness?
Who lights it?
Who steers the ship?

The poet is a mystic,
Part of an ancient order,
Traveling on a sacred journey,
To bring humans
Closer to darkness
And there must be light
To dismiss these things

It to deny poems
Existence,

.

.

.

.

.

After the poem,
There is wonder and pain
The poet's boat strikes the sandy shore
Sloshing, squishing sound of sand spreading
The poet carefully ties the boat to a post,
Takes out any stowed items,
And walks inland,
To continue searching for a soul.

Death

Breathing slows; an insignificant spark in the universe
Extinguishes.

About the Author

M. Stefan Strozier lives in New York City. He is the founder and artistic director of La Muse Venale Acting Troupe. His plays, *Guns, Shackles & Winter Coats*, *The Whales*, *The Tragedy of Abraham Lincoln*, and *The Green Game*, were performed in lengthy runs, off-off and Off-Broadway, and in the Midtown International Theatre Festival. Additionally, he has written *Belzac December Night* (a one-act play; the first of 8 plays about America), and *La Revolucion* (the first of 4 5-act plays about Mexican history; he is working on the first play in the series now, called *The New World*). He has directed seven plays and two staged reading of a musical, and produced twenty-one plays. His novels, short stories, poems, essays, plays, etceteras, are on his Web site: www.mstefanstrozier.org. He has been published in literary journals (online and in print), magazines, and newspapers. He is the founder, CEO, and publisher of World Audience Publishers, and the editor-in-chief of *audience* Magazine. His play, *La Revolucion*, is having a reading at Teatro La Tea (107 Suffolk Street, NY, NY), a non-profit theater company, on Tuesday, Jan 19th.